# MARIA FRANKLAND

# Write a Collection of Short Stories in a Year

*Everyone lives a life full of stories. Be inspired and supported to complete TEN short stories with this course.*

AUTONOMY
PRESS

This book was professionally typeset on Reedsy.
Find out more at reedsy.com

*Write a Collection of Short Stories in a Year*


*Everyone lives a life full of stories.*

# Contents

# Join my 'Keep in Touch' list!

If you'd like to be kept in the loop about new books and special offers, join my 'keep in touch' list, and receive a free booklet, 'The 7 S.E.C.R.E.T.S. to Achieving your Writing Dreams,' visit www.mariafrankland.co.uk

This book is derived from a year-long online course which includes video, access to an online support group, further writing tasks and examples, links to further reading and the option of one-to-one support.
See https://mariafrankland.co.uk/short-story-writing-course/for more information.

# Introduction

There are many people who aspire to produce a collection of short stories, and there is no doubt about what a huge accomplishment it is. However, many would-be writers cite 'I wouldn't know how to approach it,' or 'I never finish anything I start' as reasons why they never begin.

This book has been derived from an originally class-taught and now an online course, which has been tried and tested by many writers and ensured that they go from the planning processes through to the hugely enjoyable creation of story after story, towards completion of their all-important collection.

This book, as well as supporting the creation of your story collection, will develop your craft as a writer. In addition, it will give you the tools you will need to polish your first drafts until they are good enough to publish. I write this as multi-published author, and as a creative writing teacher with an MA in Creative Writing.

There are publications that promise a completed collection in less time than a year, but speaking from experience, I know that a year is a realistic ambition. You will complete at least nine short stories in different genres over the duration of the year, and maintain a regular reading habit. You will write in genres you may not have previously tried, which is great for becoming a more 'rounded' writer – exploring what you enjoy and perhaps eliminating what you don't enjoy as much.

Within each genre of writing, we will look closely at character-isation, setting, plot, structure and all the general components of creating a successful short story. Within each genre, we will also look at story elements, such as how to create a fast pace when writing crime fiction or how to create anticipation and excitement when writing for children.

I have divided the book into thirty sections with a view to a fortnight being spent on each, once you have completed the introductory section. Of course, you can approach and complete each section at a pace that suits you. Where I use examples to exemplify a technique, I either use my own writing, or signpost you towards something freely available online.

Underpinning this book is the requirement to complete at least one story every six weeks, this will result in a full size collection in a year.

Completion of your collection might be the dream and I promise you, the feeling of holding your published book in your hands is truly amazing. But I implore you to remember in those moments when it gets tough, that the journey is as rewarding as the destination. So enjoy every minute, and I look forward to helping you all the way from planning to publication.

# Flash Fiction

Welcome to the start of your exciting journey as a short story writer! I can't wait to support you from beginning to end and to ensure that my guidance helps you achieve what is probably a long-held dream. If you were taking this course in one of my face-to-face groups, or online, we would do one section every fortnight, but because this is a book, you can go as fast or as slow as you like.

Being a reader of short stories is important, as much of what you read will permeate your own writing and increase the number of 'tools' you have in your 'writer's toolbox.'

[cwb 1.1] **Write a list of the genres of fiction,** (e.g. crime.) *It might be helpful to consider the sections within a library or a bookshop.*

Think about which one you fit into or would like to fit into as a writer. Does this tie in with what you enjoy reading? This course will allow you to explore your strengths, but it will also enable you to go into unchartered territory. For example, as a crime writer, I was pleasantly surprised at my own response to writing romantic fiction and science fiction!

[cwb 1.2] **What is the essence of a 'good' story?** Write a list of 'ingredients' that a good short story should contain. These will become apparent as we proceed.

**What is flash fiction?** A moment in time – written for its 'bite-size satisfaction' for both reader and writer – increasing in popularity.

[cwb 1.3] **Take this first line.** *'I have not been asleep for long, when the phone rings.'*

Centre yourself in the story *prior* to writing it, using the prompts below before you begin: I always advise you to have a plan before beginning to write a story. If you know your story's path before you start, you are more likely to see it through.

**Who is receiving the call?**
  name, age, gender, etc
  Where are they?

**Who is making the call?**
  Name, age, gender, etc
  Why are they ringing? Where are they?

**What is being said?**
  Is there an issue between the characters? Paraphrase the conversation that will take place

**How are caller and receiver feeling?**
  Angry, fearful, joyous, worried

[cwb 1.4] **Once you have your notes**, draft a piece of flash fiction with a beginning, middle and an end in no more than 500 words. Use the given starting line and remember you are narrating a single event – a snapshot in time. Try to include as many elements of effective story as possible, (Conflict, intrigue, emotional connection, etc.)

Don't worry about spelling, punctuation or grammar at this first draft stage and don't edit anything yet. The first draft is simply you, telling yourself the story. This first writing task is just about you 'having a go.' You can return to do further editing at a later point in the course.

**Also:**

1. Buy yourself a folder to keep any notes and your work in order.
2. Buy yourself a 'special' A4 notebook and pen which you will keep only for your writing – make it a hardback one with a design you love.
3. Begin carrying a notebook and pen around with you – writers notice things. You never know when you will overhear a conversation or see something, perhaps in the landscape or a potentially interesting 'character' that could be the spark of something.

# Supernatural 1

For most of the genres we will explore as we progress through the course, we will spend three sections on each – with the exception of children's picture book. The first section will concentrate on exploration of the genre and the planning of your story.

The second section will invite you to continue drafting your first draft, stopping short of your ending, and will also focus on an element of writing skill. Then the third section within each genre will invite you to write your ending and edit your story.

One question I am often asked is *how long should a short story be.* The answer to that is anything from the aforementioned flash fiction to 10,000 words. The normal length, however seems to be around the 1,500 to 2,000 word mark. Apart from when you write the crime fiction story, I am not going to define your story length - I want you to find your own natural word count!

[cwb 2.1] **Write a list of words that come to mind when you think about the supernatural.** At least fifteen!

[cwb 2.2] **Choose your 'best' five** and use these words, in order, to write a 'spooky' short piece.

**What does a supernatural story need?** Here are some initial thoughts:

A ghost, tension, sense of unknown, mystery, fear, atmosphere, darkness, an element of wrongdoing, to be rooted in the human realm, back story, rich description, noises and other sensory details, paranormal activity, suspense, entrapment. *This is not an exhaustive list!*

**You are going to plan your own supernatural story**, working through the prompts offered below. If you are struggling to think of a story 'premise,' choose one of these:

- A dead man returns to his marital home to make his wife and her new 'lover' aware that he is still around.
- A recently dead and controlling wife doesn't want her formerly 'henpecked' husband to enjoy his new-found freedom.
- A murdered person wants to lead those that matter to the truth.
- A deceased elderly person doesn't want someone else living in their much-loved home.

[cwb 2.3] **Responding to the following questions will offer some initial ideas for your story:**

**Backstory of Ghost and main character**
   Who is the ghost?

What were they like in life?
What did they do?
What did they want?
How did they die?
What do they want now they're dead?
Who are the other character(s)?
What do the other character(s) want?

## Atmosphere

Where will the 'encounter' happen?
What are the secrets of the setting? (Rumours, stories)
What things are happening to suggest a 'haunting?'
What is the ghost's reason to be there? What is their connection?
What are the other character(s) reasons to be there?

## Encounter

What happens?
How does the ghost manifest itself?
Where? When?
What physical and emotional sensations are invoked?

## Climax/Resolution

What becomes of the character(s)? Do they achieve what they want over the story?
How does it change them?
What becomes of the ghost?

## What elements do we need for a good story opening?

Again, this isn't an exhaustive list but should be kept in mind as you write your own story opening.

Straight into some action or dialogue, meeting the main character right away, knowing immediately what genre you are writing in, no heavy description, creating an emotional involvement, and creating intrigue about what's going on.

These points will be expanded on more fully as we proceed.

[cwb 2.4] **Write your opening paragraph.**

[cwb 2.5] **Bullet point a rough progression** of how your story might continue. Get as far as you can with this.

Enjoy the process of giving your imagination free rein. Really let it loose and remember, this first draft stage is the fun and creative part. Don't try to edit anything yet – there will be plenty of time for that later. In the next section, you will continue writing your story from the first paragraph.

# Supernatural 2

*Death of the Author* is a literary term, which means that a reader is so immersed in the story they are reading, that they become almost unaware they are reading a piece of fiction that a writer has created.

They are literally *living in the story,* within the settings and amongst the characters the writer has created. This level of engagement will be so intense, they will lose track of their own existence and simply keep turning the pages.

What you are aiming for is to engross your reader to the point where they are reading when they should be sleeping, or missing their bus stop!

Create a story they are 'sad' to finish – one where they will miss the characters afterwards. Here are some tips on how to do that.

- Hook them into your story straight away. Create a compelling opening.
- Create a setting they can imagine. Make it atmospheric and drip feed sensory information through your narrative.

- Go easy on the speech tags. (Exclaimed, shouted, yelled, etc) They jar a reader from your story. Rather 'show' which character is speaking. e.g. "I just can't take it in." Richard accepted the tissue and sank onto the chair, instead of, "I just can't take it in," sobbed Richard.
- Don't use too many adverbs – use a stronger verb instead. Instead of *Mark walked quietly to the door*, use *Mark crept to the door*.
- Use adjectives sparingly and never place two together – where you can, 'show' your adjective, so instead of saying, *he was a tall man*, show him stooping below a doorframe.
- Allow reading to be an active process. Don't tell the reader *everything*. Allow them to fill in gaps and make inferences. So, if you were writing about a hospital appointment, they wouldn't necessarily need to know about the journey and the waiting room or the full conversation with the receptionist, just the bits that keep the story moving forwards.

There is an unsigned contract between writer and reader. You, as the writer, promise to give your reader an immersive and entertaining reading experience, and they promise to read your story to the end. But only if they can *lose* themselves in it, otherwise you will lose *them*.

You have already written your story opening and may have the rest of your story loosely mapped out in bullet points. Don't worry if this 'mapping out' is quite vague at this stage. You may have around five or six bullet points which will become the scenes which make up your story. Firstly re-read your opening paragraph to re-centre yourself in your story.

Then, take your first bullet pointed paragraph for which you are going to write the next scene after the opening. Do a rough outline sketch first, taking it from beginning to end.

[cwb3.1] **Take your own second scene**, (after your story opening) and break it down into 4 or 5 'sub bullet points.'

- Beginning of scene 2
- Then
- Then
- Then
- Ending of scene 2

[cwb 3.2] **Now write your scene**, putting flesh on the bones of your 'scene skeleton.'

[cwb 3.3-3.10] **Do the same with your other planned bullet points**, (which will become individual scenes,) fleshing them out first, as above, and then writing them out in full.

I advocate doing this stage in longhand, as I find this is a more 'creative' process. Although all writers do things differently, I find it best to leave typing until the second draft.

Try not to edit anything at this stage – you can do this later. Enjoy the creation. As I said in the last section, this first draft stage is you, the writer, telling the story to yourself.

Get your story to where you have it as a first draft, up to the point of writing the final scene. Don't write it yet! We will look at ending your story in the next section.

Remember that reading will give you extra tools in your development as a writer. Often what you enjoy reading is what you will enjoy writing as well. As we progress through the course, I advise you to read in the genre we are working in. For this supernatural genre, I recommend *Click Clack the Rattlebag,* by Neil Gaiman, freely available online to read or listen to.

# Supernatural 3

Let's start with a few ideas of what a short story might need, (particularly a supernatural one,) to bring it to a resolution:

- Allow the ghost (or similar) to find peace and rest.
- End with a comeuppance.
- Write a satisfying or happy ending.
- Ensure a contrast with how the story began.
- Answer vital questions that may have been raised throughout the story.
- Allow the reader to infer what may happen next.
- A bad ending is s/he woke up, and it was all a dream! But I am sure you will not need me to tell you that!

To re-orientate yourself within your story, read back what you have written so far. You may want to read your piece aloud, (*remember, no editing yet!*) It can be particularly powerful to read the 'encounter' scene aloud again.

You should now have the first draft of your story up to the point of drafting your resolution. Think about how you would like your reader to feel at the end of your story, (e.g. relieved, satisfied, saddened, moved, inspired.)

[cwb 4.1] **Use bullet points to plan the progression of your ending.**

[cwb 4.2] **Now draft your ending.**

Next comes the all-important editing stage. As a writer, you may be aware of a tendency to do particular things in your writing that need editing later. For example, the overuse of particular words, or the inclusion of too many adjectives in your early drafts. My greatest faux pas are the overuse of 'a bit' or 'a little,' and I use the word 'just' just too often.

[cwb 4.3] **Make a list of things you realise you do when looking back over your first draft.**

We will continue to revisit editing as we work through the genres, but below are some introductory ideas. Many of the concepts mentioned will be looked at in more depth soon:

- See where you can lose adjectives. (Show, rather than tell.)
- See where you can lose adverbs. (Use a stronger verb)
- Check for repetition.
- Check for the overuse of words and word phrases.
- Check for use of superfluous words. (e.g. very, so, just, really, that)
- Read aloud (especially dialogue,) to check for flow and authenticity.
- Check you have 'played out' your scenes, using dialogue and character action, rather than just describing them.
- Check for inconsistency. (e.g. character details.)

It is best to allow your story to 'go cold' for a day or two before editing. Use the list you devised in the last task of things to look for and apply it to your story.

If you have handwritten your first draft, now type up your second draft. If it is already typed, correct your story to produce a second draft. You will produce a third draft later in the course.

I hope you will love editing as much as I do!

# Science Fiction 1

First, a reminder to remember to read in the genre you are writing in. And let me direct you to one of the greats, freely available online: The Watery Place by Isaac Asimov.

### *What is Science Fiction?*

The core of science fiction lets us run free with the idea of *'what if?'* dealing with potential technologies of the future, where it is often set. We can also set it in space, in different worlds or other universes. Often it is rooted in philosophy.

It is a genre which projects scientific ideas to imagined extremes and can explore potential new technologies, along with the implications if they were to come about – positive and negative. It often deals with social science and politics.

Science fiction usually includes a human element and teaches us as writers and readers to think about possibilities which manipulate science, whilst addressing human values. This can include ethical considerations around 'if' something is 'right.' (e.g. genetic modification.)

The genre is now often known as 'speculative fiction' because it explores ways of life that might become possible with scientific advances.

### What is the difference between science fiction and fantasy?

Science Fiction deals with science and therefore is not beyond the realm of possibility, whereas fantasy is. However, there is much overlap between the two genres and they are often shelved together in bookshops and libraries. Lots of stories 'cross over' between science fiction and fantasy. For example, *Avatar* is set in a fantastical land, but the spaceship component offers the sci-fi element.

In this genre, the known laws of the universe are not broken, (e.g. the law of gravity,) whereas in fantasy, magic exists which can break any 'law' it wants. We will have a closer look at fantasy later.

I never considered myself as a reader of science fiction until I began to research the various sub-genre of science fiction, (e.g. dystopia.) So this is a great starting place:

### What are the sub genres of the genre?

**Dystopia** fiction warns of future consequences if the world doesn't change its actions, or becomes more corrupt. It must have a scientific premise or angle – but not all dystopia is scientific and may be more speculative. e.g. *1984* George Orwell.

**Utopia** fiction aims to empower us to create a better future. It presents a world in which everything is perfect and harmonious. e.g. *Men Like Gods* HG Wells.

**Time Travel** fiction journeys backwards and forwards through time to explore what could be and what could have been different. e.g. *A Christmas Carol* Charles Dickens or *Hitchhiker's Guide to the Galaxy,* ( a five book 'trilogy') Douglas Adams.

**Spaceflight** fiction is set whilst the characters are travelling through space e.g. *The Gap Cycle* (a five-book series) Stephen Donaldson.

**Extra Terrestrial Life/Aliens** fiction is set in space or other universes or explores alien life existing on earth. e.g. *Trouble on Triton* Samuel R. Delany.

**Apocalyptic/Post-Apocalyptic** fiction explores disaster/the end of the world and any life force beyond that. e.g. *The Stand* Stephen King.

**Theological** fiction considers deep religious aspects and what may lie beyond life. e.g. *Space Trilogy* C S Lewis.

**Super Human** fiction explores characters with super human attributes such as immortality or invisibility e.g. *Pandora's Star* Peter Hamilton.

**Under Sea** fiction is set in underwater universes e.g. *Starfish* Peter Watts.

[cwb 5.1] **Consider what sub-genre you might be most interested in as both a reader, and as a writer**.

[cwb 5.2] **Settle on a concept of the science fiction genre that interests you**. (e.g. the ability to travel through time, the theme of immortality or the theme of being able to experience a parallel universe)

[cwb 5.3] **Pose your own 'what ifs.'** Here are some ideas if you need help with generating an initial concept:

- Write about a magic power you gain for a day (e.g. telepathy, invisibility, capability to time travel.) How do you use it?
- Write about a world where a patient is woken up from a long sleep when a cure for their terminal illness had been found.
- It's one hundred years from now. You're immortal. What is the world like?
- Write about a character who has cloned him or herself.
- What if we could connect/disconnect to one another by Bluetooth?

Remember the only pre-requisites for science fiction are:

- what you are writing will be fictional.
- it will be within the perceived realm of possibility and scientific development.

[cwb 5.4] **Taking one of the above ideas, or one of your own, flesh out an initial plan:**

**Who?** *The characters,* these might include aliens, animals, robots, or other life force. Make sure you still make them relatable.

**When?** *The era, likely duration and time of your story.* Will it travel between time?

**Where?** *Will your story be set on earth, in space, another planet or somewhere else?* Stick to general descriptions – readers may not want to be 'bogged down' with the exact mechanics of how your imaginary world works and there isn't too much space for it within the confines of a short story.

**Why?** *What questions would you like to raise?* How might you want to leave your reader feeling? Do you want to leave your reader with an overall message?

**What?** *What will happen? What is your story trying to achieve?* What journey will it take?

- Opening and Introduction:
- Next:
- Then:
- Climax of Story or Twist:
- Resolution and Ending:

[cwb 5.5] **You could plot these notes onto a story arc, which is how a short story should be shaped.** By this, I mean that stories are firstly opened and introduced, then there is a progressive rise in action - the upward direction of the arc - which may have peaks and troughs as it builds towards the climax of the story - the apex of the arc -. The story then falls – the downward direction of the arc- towards its resolution.

A story is constructed of smaller scenes that make the story. It often makes for a stronger story if your individual scenes follow the same story arc approach as the overall story. I will introduce more planning devices as you work through the sections of this book.

Now for the exciting bit! You have your plan and you are going to begin writing your science fiction story.

## [cwb 5.6] Now write your story opening

You might want to look at some story openings from other science fiction stories first. Consider what you like (or not!) about the opening. Again, allow me to point you towards *1984, The Time Traveller's Wife* and *Something Coming Through.*

You may wish to refer to the ingredients for a good story opening from the supernatural section.

**Remember – just write – no editing. (Not yet!)**

# Science Fiction 2

Before you progress further with your story, let us take a look at using language to enhance your writing, as it is one of the many vital tools in every writer's toolbox. Here are some tips:

**Using Metaphor** A metaphor is when we say something <u>is</u> something else. For example, *hope is a fragile seed,* or *his life was a cloudy day.*

**Use of Simile** A simile is like a metaphor in that it still offers a comparison between two 'likenesses,' but uses the words 'like' or 'as' to conjure the representation. For example, *something gave way in him like a burning ember,* or *as excited as a Christmas Eve child.*

**Avoidance of Cliché** They are easily used, which doesn't matter in your first draft, but make sure you identify and replace them in your second draft, e.g. as *sharp as a knife, or he was like a cat on a hot tin roof.*

**Use of Effective Imagery** We can use language to ensure we create atmosphere in an immersive, visual, auditory, and physical sense. Much contemporary fiction aims to do this, using as few sentences and words as possible, to achieve the 'page-turning and easy-reading' effect we want.

For example, *the waiting room is full. Everyone is staring at us from their plastic seats which are bolted to the floor. Apart from the whitewashed walls, all is green. And the stench of body odour is threatening to snatch my breath away.*

**Variety of Language** We have a huge repertoire of words that can say the same thing but offer more power to our writing. For example, instead of saying, *he walked down the path quickly*, we can say, *he dashed down the path.*

**Avoidance of Repetition** Don't worry too much about this at first draft stage, but it is something to keep in mind. Writers often overuse the same words or phrases, for example:

- A word I often overuse is *hope, hoping or hopeful.*
- A phrase I often overuse is *if only he could turn back time, go back in time, turn the clock back, etc.*

A thesaurus or the synonyms function in your word processing programme can offer alternatives to words.

**Other ways you can increase your vocabulary**

- Learn how language works – e.g. the roots and suffixes of words.
- Keep resources like a thesaurus and dictionary close to hand whilst writing.
- Read widely, new vocabulary will naturally assimilate into

your own writing.
- Be open in your daily life to new words – look up ones you hear, then use them in your writing.

It is now time to continue with the planning and first drafting of your story, using the elements of your already drawn initial plan. Using the story arc as your planning approach, take each of your scenes one-by-one, and plot them out before writing. You have already written your opening.

[cwb 6.1] **Take the next scene from your overall story,** and sub plot it onto a story arc. When you have this 'skeleton' of your scene, it will be easier for you to write the first draft.

[cwb 6.2-6.10] **Repeat the process with further scenes in your story,** stopping short of planning or writing your ending.

If possible, whilst you are writing your science fiction story, include at least one of each of the following techniques: One metaphor, one simile, the use of imagery and the intention towards use of a variety of language with the aid of a thesaurus and/or a book of synonyms.

# Science Fiction 3

By now you will be itching to write the ending of your science fiction short story! One of the most exciting things about being a writer is that the characters and the stories start to live within you and will not leave you alone.

Read your story through to the point at which you have got it so far. You should have written it to where you are about to write the ending.

[cwb 7.1] **Plot out your ending**, using the 'story arc' approach that you have been using to plan your previous scenes.

[cwb 7.2] **Using this plan, write the first draft of your ending scene.**

It is now time to type your work as a second draft or amend your current version if it is already on screen, keeping the following tips to hand as you edit.

These are all tips you can continue to use in each of your stories throughout the course.

## Tips for Editing

As I have already mentioned, we should not carry out editing when initially drafting our work.

Use these tips when editing – a scene of your story at a time:

- Decide whether your scene has started in the right place. Writers often launch in too early, giving too much explanation or backstory instead of going straight in at a point of action.
- Check every word is the best it can be. Use a thesaurus to help. Or the 'synonyms' function on your computer. Every word counts.
- Beware of 'overwriting.' Of being too wordy. Less is more, so go easy with the adjectives.
- Ensure consistency of viewpoint, of character details, etc.
- Editing does not mean only 'cutting' things – bits you've 'skipped over' may also need expansion.
- Eliminate superfluous words. Make a list of these. The words you throw in, out of habit, like *very* and *just*. Or phrases like *began to* or *started to.*
- Avoid being too wordy. Don't use two words when one will say the same thing. If two adjectives are similar, pick the best one and lose the other.
- Remember that reading should be an active process – enable the reader to 'fill in gaps' themselves and infer information.
- Know what your story is trying to achieve, its message, its journey. Has it done this?

## Then:

1. Print your story and annotate the paper version with a pen. You will notice things on the page you have not seen on the computer screen.
2. You should also read it aloud – this will highlight issues with flow and repetition of words or phrases.
3. If possible, get someone else to read it. Another pair of eyes will often spot mistakes and also be able to comment on content.
4. Unnecessary words and phrases can find their way into our writing and drag it down. We should write as concisely as possible for our meaning to be understood. This shouldn't affect a writer's style and voice.

# Romance 1

I hope you did not think you were going to take a short story course without writing a romantic story! Even if this is the only one that you ever write, it will have pushed you out of your comfort zone as a writer and you will learn something. This is one of the jobs of this course – to invite you to try things, you may not have tried otherwise. Of course, you might love writing romantic fiction, and will find this a breeze!

So, let us find our way into this genre of story by considering why readers turn to romantic fiction in the first place:

- For escapism.
- For the enjoyment of the 'happy ever after element.'
- To experience the depths of the emotion alongside the characters.
- To deal with identifiable issues within their own relationships.
- For the bond they create with the characters.
- To live out the 'fantasy' of the often 'heroic' love interest

To fulfil the expectations of your readers, you should ensure your story contains emotional depth, and offers characters that can be connected with. An issue can be explored, a fantasy lived out and I would generally advise a happy ending, but as mentioned in the list below, love story endings can also be tragic – think Romeo and Juliet! So now let us consider what some of the ingredients for a romantic story might be:

- Emotion and feelings. (Vitally important.) This can be an exploration of darker human emotions, (Fear, pain, disappointment, jealousy.)
- A building of tension throughout the story.
- An obstacle getting in the way of a 'happy ever after,' – something keeping the characters apart. This provides the conflict.
- A feeling that love can overcome anything.
- Relatable situations.
- An atmospheric setting.
- Lots of dialogue.
- Avoidance of cliché.
- Happy-ever-after or a tragedy.
- Backstory and memories.

As I already suggested, readers often read romance for the 'happy ever after,' and the triumph over adversity element of story. One of the best love story writers of all time was Anton Chekov whose short stories are available online.

A primary human need is to feel a sense of belonging, as such, this is a deep-seated desire in many. Most people want to feel the depth of connection that a human relationship offers. Reading a romance story allows readers to experience that depth of feeling through the characters they connect with.

Of course, the journey to happy ever after is never a straightforward one, and that's what offers the intrigue and readability for many a romantic fiction.

Now all that has been said, it is time to get to work!

**Start by finding pictures of two potential characters –** your story protagonist, through whose eyes the story will be told, and their love interest.

I suggest you use a character-driven approach for the writing of this story, so you will get to know your characters and what is behind their situation. Do this first for your main character, and then again for their love interest.

[cwb 8.1] **The following prompts will help you achieve this:**

1. Character's Name/Age:
2. Occupation:
3. Home/Family Information:
4. Interests:
5. A talent they have been told they possess:
6. Divulge a secret they have:
7. One thing they did yesterday:
8. One thing they must do tomorrow:
9. Biggest Dream:
10. Greatest Fear:
11. First Love:
12. Most romantic thing they have ever done:

Not all of this information will make it into your story, but the better you know your characters before you bring them to the page, the more your reader will connect with them.

[cwb 8.2] **Now you have become acquainted with your characters, it is time to bring them together.**

Use the following questions to support this process:

- How do your characters know each other? Where did they meet/will they meet?
- Is one in pursuit of their relationship more than the other?
- If applicable, how do people around them feel about them being together?
- What is impeding them being together? This is the crux of the story!
- Any other details relating to the situation of your characters.

Excellent – well done! Now for the next exciting bit – the opening of your romantic story. You will use a scene by scene approach for this genre, rather than planning a whole story overview, as with your previous stories.

This allows your story to unfold and occur naturally just as any real-life romance would! You should bring in the knowledge you have gained so far on what a good story opening needs – flick back a few pages to refresh your memory.

As well as only planning scene by scene, you will use another planning technique. Instead of a story arc, you will use the scene card approach. Imagine the following headings being placed within a table on a card – you can make some cards for this.

You will need the following information:

- Scene heading:
- Time of day/date/era:
- Characters Involved:
- Setting:
- Other Information:
- Scene Introduction:
- Next:
- Then:
- Conclusion:

[cwb 8.3] **Use the above to plan your own opening scene.**

[cwb 8.4] **And then write it out.**

Ensure you introduce both your characters and offer some information about what is standing in the way of them being together.

Enjoy!

# Romance 2

Dialogue is a vital component within *any* story genre, but even more so within a romantic story.

It exists to:

- Reveal characters' relationships to each other. Relationships can be 'shown' rather than 'told' by what the characters say to one another.
- Offer information about a character. It can offer details about where they live, their background and social standing and what sort of person they are.
- Move the story forwards. Dialogue brings the narrative to life. It enables the reader to visualise what is taking place and to hear the character's voice. Furthermore, it breaks up blocks of narration. Many readers are put off by a page full of dense text.
- Increase the tension. Drama is created by what is said, and how it is said, although, what is not said can also add to the tension. Sometimes a character's 'internal thought' can be placed alongside dialogue. Only that of your viewpoint character though!

## 'Rules' when writing dialogue

1. New speaker – new line.
2. Speech marks go on the outside of punctuation marks.
3. Try not to overuse speech tags, (replied, asked, said, etc,) and when you do use them, keep them simple, (no need for murmured, screamed, extrapolated!) Too much could jar the reader out of your story.
4. Use character action to break up the dialogue. This is important. You can show anger, excitement, etc. by what a character does and how they do it. *(e.g. Sarah slammed the book onto the table. "I can't do it!")* Using this method also shows the reader who is speaking without having to rely on speech tags.
5. Go easy on the adverbs, (happily, slowly, etc.) Rather show *how* something is being said through the actual words and the way the character is acting.
6. Keep it interesting. Avoid any mundane conversation that doesn't move your story along.
7. Read your dialogue aloud to check it flows. (At editing stage – don't worry about this yet!)

## What do you like/dislike about the following two short examples of dialogue?

*"Why didn't you say this before?" Wendy couldn't believe what she was hearing.*

*"To be honest, I didn't think we'd end up being this serious." Joe placed his cup back on its saucer.*

*Wendy stepped towards Joe and reached for his hand. "Can't we talk about this?"*

35

*Joe brushed her hand aside and turned from her. "I thought I could cope with him living with us. But I can't. It's him or me."*

*"But Joe!" Wendy sat beside him. "You can't ask me to get rid of my dog for you! You can't."*

*"I'm not keen on dogs," said Joe.*

*"Why not," asked Wendy.*

*"They smell and they lose hair," replied Joe.*

*"I've got a dog," asserted Wendy.*

*"Have you?" answered Joe.*

*"Yes," replied Wendy.*

*"Then we can't be together after all," said Joe.*

*"Why not?" asked Wendy.*

*"Because I'm not keen on dogs," said Joe.*

So, as you continue with your romantic short story, be sure to use dialogue to help move it along. Enable your reader to experience what is being said and how it is being said between your characters. For example, don't say, *Wendy* and Joe had an argument, rather allow the argument to play out. This is 'show, don't tell' at its best.

Now write your story opening and be ready to progress with subsequent scenes. But before starting to progress the romance, read back through your character outlines and the story development notes you have already made. Also, read through your story opening again.

You are going to allow the story between your characters to unfold organically, (just like in real life,) using the 'scene cards approach' to plan each scene before you write it.

I have purposefully not asked you to plan out an overview of the entire story this time, to give you the opportunity to see how you write when planning as you go along, rather than before you start.

However, by now, you will be getting to know your characters and their situation, therefore you may already have a good idea of the journey they are going to take.

As you plan and write each scene, keep the information in mind from the last section - *why readers read romance,* and *what ingredients a love story should contain.*

**Continue to write your romantic story, planning each scene** [cwb 9.1-5] **and then writing each scene in first draft** [cwb 9.2-5] until you get to where you are about to write your final scene.

# Romance 3

Your story should be at the point where you are about to write your end scene. You will have used a scene-by-scene approach, planning each scene, then drafting it. I hope you are enjoying writing your romantic story!

You have allowed the situation so far between your characters to unfold organically, using the scene card approach to plan each scene before you write it.

Maybe you still have no idea how your story will end. This section will concentrate on your ending, then editing your story.

Read over all your notes so far, (your character inventions and those on what brought them together.) Then read the draft of the story you have written so far. There will be things that will immediately stand out to you that need editing but resist the temptation – for now! You should finish the story before you begin any editing.

I have purposefully laboured the points for you to reread your notes and your draft story. Do so again, so you really know, and you can feel your characters; inside and out. Which brings us to the ending... Let us first consider how to end a short story, in regard to a romantic story.

- Think about how you want your reader to feel when they get to the end, (sad, uplifted, hopeful, etc.)
- Could there be a twist, something the reader will not see coming?
- A happy ending?
- A tragic ending?
- An ending that leaves the reader to draw their own conclusions?
- An ending that gives a message or a moral?
- An ending that provides complete resolution and closure?
- Lastly, ensure that the characters have evolved in some way between the start and the end of the story.

[cwb 10.1] **Use the scene card planning approach to plan your end scene, then write your first draft.** [cwb 10.2]

**And now for the editing part...**

[cwb 10.3] **What clichés can you bring to mind that are commonly found in love stories?** (e.g. pounding heart.) A cliché is an overused statement or phrase.

[cwb 10.4] **Can you replace any of these clichés with something more original?** Are you aware of using any yourself in your own story? Omit or substitute any you have included in your first draft as you edit your story.

Use the editing checklist from the science-fiction section as you complete your second draft. After this second draft is complete, put it aside - you can return it to later in the course.

# Writing for Children

People often think that writing for children is easy. However, there is a lot that needs to be considered when writing for such a discerning audience, as follows:

- The creation of a character that children will be able to relate to.
- The dealing with of an issue or situation that children will be able to hang their life experiences on.
- Creating something that is enjoyable to read.
- Writing something that presents a suitable amount of challenge.
- Remembering an adult is more likely to choose your book and then share it with a child.

It's helpful to have a child in mind that you will write for. It is also helpful to look at a variety of children's picture books first, to become familiar with the typical language and layout.

**What different genres of children's stories are there?**

Just as with adult books, there are many genres of children's books, e.g. ghost, adventure, humour, fantasy, issue-based.

## What 'ingredients' do you need for a good children's story?

Again, like adult books, there are certain expectations, e.g. a relatable character, escapism, a problem to be solved, an adventure, a happy ending.

So now, you are going to plan, then write a 'picture book,' of 500-1000 words for children around the age 4-7. It is useful to consider what you enjoyed reading as a child? Who was your favourite character? What was your favourite book and why? Your thoughts here might inform the sort of story you will write.

[cwb 11.1] **Respond to the prompts below to invent your main character**. You could work from a picture or invent your character from your imagination. If it is animalistic, give it human qualities and emotions. Give your imagination free rein and don't 'overthink' each decision. The more you plan, the easier your story will be to write but don't worry if you end up deviating. Characters sometimes have the tendency to go their own way!

- Name/age:
- Appearance:
- Family information:
- Their favourite place:
- Two things they did yesterday:
- One thing they must do tomorrow:
- The most special thing they own:
- A talent they possess:

- Happiest memory:
- What makes them angry?
- What makes them laugh?
- What is their biggest dream?
- Internal Monologue: Now have your character introduce themselves, as though they are speaking.

[cwb 11.2] **Choose a picture to help you, or invent your own setting.** Imagine you are writing a postcard from your setting to someone who has never visited. Use lots of sensory information.

[cwb 11.3] **Next, jot some notes in response to the following three questions.** None of this is set in stone, but meant to provide a starting point for you.

- What does your character want to achieve over the course of the story?
- What is standing in their way?
- What other characters will be in your story?

[cwb 11.4] **Plan your story before you start writing.**

- How will your story begin?
- And then what will happen?
- What will happen next?
- What will happen then to make it really exciting?
- How will your story end?
- How do you want your reader to feel after they have finished reading your story?
- What message would you like to convey to your reader?

**Use your plan to write your first draft.** Go from beginning to end without editing. Keep your 'target reader' in mind as you write.

You may also have some thoughts on illustrations. Perhaps you can undertake the illustrations yourself, (unlike me!) Or you may know someone you can collaborate with. Most children's publishers would just require the story from you at this stage and would link your work with an illustrator of their own choosing. However, some welcome the submission of illustrations, along with your manuscript.

After you have written the first draft, transfer this handwritten draft onto the computer, using the earlier editing checklist.

If you have enjoyed the process of writing for this age group, something to bear in mind is that children, (and publishers,) are more likely to be 'won over' with a series!

And if this is the only children's story you have ever written then consider yourself well and truly pushed out of your writing pigeon hole!

# Crime 1

It gives me great pleasure to introduce the genre I write and predominantly read in! Crime fiction. It is one of the best-selling genres in adult fiction, probably because it provides an immersive experience that is thrilling, gripping and page-turning.

It allows readers into normally unseen places such as courts and police interview rooms whilst offering an insight into the darker side of life and the worst of human emotion and relationships.

The guessing game is another enjoyable element. Readers enjoy the process of 'whodunnit' and want to be shocked when the truth is finally revealed.

The term crime fiction is a broad umbrella to what exists beneath it. Its ever-growing popularity has created many sub-genres such as police procedurals, courtroom dramas, cosy crime (suburban or domestic,) hard-boiled (violent aftermath,) private investigation, spy and psychological thrillers. *You might wish to do some further research into the sub genres.* When you find the sub genre of domestic thriller...well...see you there!

Within these headings are further sub-headings for example, thrillers could be medical, military, legal, etc. The most popular crime that is committed in crime fiction is murder, but what defines a crime story is - it contains a crime - any crime; so kidnap, theft, terrorism, fraud, arson, vandalism are other crimes that feature. *You might like to add to this list.*

A perpetrator of a crime would not commit a crime, whether premeditated or in the moment **without a motive**. Criminal activity can be driven by greed, jealousy, boredom, revenge or insanity, to name but a few. *Again, you might want to add to this list.*

As a crime writer, you must be accurate when writing scenes, especially those that could be challenged by a professional. For example, in a UK courtroom, a judge does not use a gavel nor does anyone for the defence jump up, shouting *objection.* You are best to 'skirt around' a situation, than to portray it incorrectly.

Thankfully, much of what we could ever need to research is available on the internet. As a writer of psychological thrillers, I often worry about the search history on my computer. I know my husband does!

[cwb 12.1] **To begin, you are going to plot your crime, addressing the what, why, when, where and who of your story.** Choose a crime that most interests you and then a motive for the 'what' and 'why.' Make your initial notes as detailed as possible. Go with your gut instinct for each prompt and remember that nothing is set in stone – characters do have the habit of deviating from what we have planned and that is fine.

- **What?** The crime that will be committed
- **Why?** What is the motive?
- **When?** Era and time span. Time of year or day.
- **Where?** Area. Location. Make some sensory notes on a possible opening setting.
- **Who?** The perpetrators, victims, and accomplices. We will get to know them in more detail shortly.

The general rule of thumb is the shorter the story, the fewer the main characters. Differing from the romance genre when I asked you to find pictures of your characters, this time you are going to invent their appearance through visualisation.

**I would now like you to create your perpetrator** [cwb 12.2] **and victim** [cwb 12.3] using the prompts offered below.

Name/Age:

Occupation:

Appearance:

Home/Family:

Three facts about their 'past:'

A positive character trait:

A negative character trait:

Interior Monologue: *Have your character introduce themselves ...*

You should also consider what research might be necessary before, and as you write your story. Crime fiction commonly contains scenes to do with forensics, police activity, and court procedure.

It is important to get this right. Perhaps you know someone who works within one of these fields who will read over your work or if not, the internet can provide much of what you will need to clarify.

[cwb 12.4] **Once you have considered the prompts below, you will be well placed to begin to write:**

- Is any research necessary prior to beginning your story?
- At what point in your story will the crime occur?
- Will the crime be planned?
- What events will lead up to the crime being carried out?
- How will the perpetrator be feeling physically and emotionally as they commit the crime?
- Will he or she feel any remorse afterwards?
- Will the crime be 'successfully' carried out or will it 'go wrong?'
- What events will occur after the crime?
- Will anyone else be affected by the crime?
- Will the perpetrator be caught and/or punished?
- Notes (other things that immediately spring to mind – phrases, images, viewpoint, tense, twist, structure.)

**As always, when you are working in a particular genre, try also to read it.**

I would be doing myself a disservice if I didn't recommend a novella-size crime story I have written, A Life for A Life, freely available by visiting www.autonomypress.co.uk and entering your email address.

This will also place you on my 'keep in touch' list for readers.

# Crime 2

Pace plays an important role in crime fiction. When used well, we can keep the reader on the edge of their seat before being offered a reprieve. This variation of pace often determines whether they will continue to read a story, or not.

**Definition of Pace** In any genre, narrative pace determines the speed at which the writer takes a reader through a story. It relies on a combination of mood and emotion as these elements play out in the dialogue, setting and action.

For example, Dan Brown's *The DaVinci Code* has a much faster pace than Elizabeth Gilbert's *Eat, Pray, Love.*

The pace of a story can vary, for example, the opening pace may feel totally different from that of the story's climax.

**Upping the Pace** Fast action and rapid sequencing increase the pace. These narrative elements make the reader want to keep reading to see what happens to the story's protagonist. Action sequences containing little dialogue and minimal thoughts from the characters best create the fast action.

Rapid sequencing is where moments happen one right after the other, helping the pace of the story feel faster. Where dialogue is used, it should be short and snappy, and not interwoven with too much character internal thought and detail.

**Slowing It Down** Narrative passages that contain more detail, establishing setting and containing longer sentences, feel slower. This brings the pace down; it can build suspense and allows the reader to catch their breath between action sequences. Where dialogue is used, it can be more detailed and accompanied with thought and description.

**Striking a Balance** The most interesting stories contain scenes that move at different speeds. These keep the reader engaged. Juxtaposing chapters that feature description, thought and emotion, alongside others with fast-paced action sequences can strike the right balance.

### An Example of Quick Pace

I know where he lives. Connor, I mean. Easy to stalk people nowadays. The knot in my belly tightens. I swing my car around in the road and embark on the next leg of my journey. This may put my mind at rest, but probably won't. "Please. Please. Please," I whisper in the darkness. I turn the final corner. I pull up a couple of doors away, a couple of car lengths behind Meghan's VW Golf. I see the pink air freshener suspended from the mirror.

*I don't believe it.* I thump the steering wheel. The horn sounds. *Bloody hell.* The curtain twitches in one of the upstairs windows.

I feel like marching up to the door and dragging her out of there. Make her see the life she's giving up with me. I thought she cared about me. I thought we were going places. I thought – *well to hell with what I thought!* She's with him.

- Quick action and fast to read
- 'Strong' verbs – thump, swing, march, drag
- Minimal dialogue
- Short sentences
- Action rather than description

## An Example of Slow Pace

With a heavy heart, I tug my glove box open and fumble around until I find a pen and an old Asda receipt. I've got to let her know that I've been here and know about what she's doing. I write on the back of it *Thanks. What an idiot I've been. J*

I sneak to her car and tuck it under one of the wipers, hardly breathing until I'm back in the cocoon of my car again. I wish you were at home Mum. You'd tell me that it's all her loss and that someone else will snap me up soon.

I feel like crap and hope Meghan will as well when she finds that note. I start the car up and begin driving home. It's starting to get light. I can see the sun coming up behind the hills. I can't carry on like this.

- Longer sentences.
- Description.
- Internal thoughts.

- Emotions expressed are sadness and loneliness.
- Softer verbs – tuck, tug, fumble.

Now read through the notes you have so far for your crime story. When you get to the characters you invented, read the monologues you wrote *aloud* so you can hear their voices.

For the only time in this course, I'm going to suggest a word count of 1600 to guide you through your story. It is great practice to adhere to a word count, should you wish to submit your short story to an outlet like a competition or an anthology.

[cwb 13.1] **Read some crime story openings** and consider what features are included within them that are effective, for example:

- Choice of verbs and other vocabulary (e.g. creaked)
- Components included (e.g. blood, flies) – indication of genre
- Shorter sentences
- Setting Descriptions
- Introduction of character

If you have already read mine, you have one example to look at. Another one you can freely find online is *Man Walks into a Bar* by Lee Child.

[cwb 13.2] **Write your story opening.** Use one of the planning techniques we have used so far. (Bullet pointing, scene card, or scene arc.) Aim for around 200 words.

[cwb 13.3-9] **Continue with your story scene by scene-planning, then first drafting.**

Aim for a further 4 scenes of 300 words each. (An overall total of six scenes) Then you will write your resolution scene of 200 words. Stop when you are about to write the ending. *Note: 250 words is roughly one handwritten side of A4. Your total story will be around the 1600 word mark.*

**Ensure you pay attention to 'pace' in scene 3,** (when the action will be rising,) and in scene five, (when your story is reaching its climax.)

Below are some further techniques that will ensure a successful story:

**Adherence to plot** Keep in mind the protagonist's overall aim, whether the victim or the perpetrator. There will be obstacles for them along the way and the more insurmountable they are, the more of a page-turning story is ensured.

There is often not enough space within the short story structure to have too complex a plot, so limit the number of characters and sub plots you use.

**Character** Multi-dimensional characters have reasons for doing what they do. You can experiment with which character you choose for your protagonist and also experiment with whether you tell your story in first person, (me, I, my,) or third person, (he, she, him, her.)

In crime fiction, first person increases suspense as readers only know what is happening for that one character. Using a this viewpoint allows the reader more inside the character's head.

**Tense** Another decision to be experimented with. In crime fiction, telling in present tense offers more immediacy and carries the reader along with the action of the story.

**Suspense** Don't make the crime too easy to solve, so have possibilities of potential suspects or outcomes. Create as many will they/won't they moments as possible. Frustrate your reader. Within the constraints of short story, you don't have as much space for too many suspects.

**Structure** Use a balance of back story, dialogue, character action, setting, and description. Think about utilising a twist towards the end of the story. A reader should have no idea that a twist is coming but will have an 'oh yes!' moment when they recall the strategically placed clues that led them to that point.

**Cinematic Approach** Imagine an actual camera panning out before a moment of action then suddenly zooming in on it.

**Pace** A page-turner can be created by using frequent jumps from scene-to-scene, and also by using shorter sentences. Pace can be increased by using less description and less dialogue and internal thought. We can slow pace down by doing the opposite, (more dialogue, longer sentences, more description.)

**Tension** Have the protagonist stuck in a seemingly impossible situation, encountering no end of obstacles. Consider using a slow build up towards the moment of crime.

**A satisfying ending** Make it clear what crime has been committed, by who and why. Whether the perpetrator gets their 'comeuppance' is up to you!

# Crime 3

By now, you ought to have written a crime story that stops short of its ending. You will have:

- Written an opening that embodies some of the features mentioned in the previous section, and,
- Written your scenes in first draft up to the ending, adhering (if possible!) to the given word count constraints.

{cwb 14.1] Let me offer some guidance to help you plan the resolution for your story.

- In two sentences, summarise what will happen in your final scene.
- Will all the loose ends be tied up?
- Jot down two possibilities for alternative endings?
- How do you want your reader to feel after reading it?
- Consider two options: complete comeuppance or room for reader inference. (The ending left open so a reader can draw their own conclusions regarding justice or possibly 'getting away with it.')
- Is there a group of people whereby it would be acceptable for justice not to be done? (i.e. villains where the reader

could accept their killer not being punished) e.g. fanatics, misogynists, bullies, etc.

[cwb 14.2] **Use your preferred planning strategy to plan and then write your ending.**

Type up your handwritten story or if it is already typed, go over what you have typed, improving as necessary, implement the responses from the previous activity.

**Print your story out and annotate – it will look different on screen to the page.**

[cwb 14.3] **Now edit your story, taking the points below into account as you do:**

1. Does your title capture the *essence* of your story? Is it attention grabbing?
2. Have you started in the right place? Think about starting a paragraph or two earlier or later if you're unsure. Does it offer an immediate introduction to the characters and setting? Does it foreshadow events and cause intrigue?
3. Is your dialogue realistic and engaging when you read it aloud?
4. Have you adhered to your plot? Even if you have changed your story from your original plan, has your character overcome whatever was standing in his/her way?
5. Have you allowed the reader to do some work by leaving gaps in your story for them to fill themselves, clues for them to pick up and a list of possible 'suspects?
6. Is your story written in the best tense? Have you con-

sidered the effect of switching past into present or vice versa?

7. Have you told your story from the best viewpoint? Have you considered the difference it will make, if you allow the story to be told from another character's viewpoint? Is your viewpoint consistent?

8. Have you managed to create some moments when the reader will have no clue of what may come next and will be quickly page turning in order to find out?

9. Can you imagine your crime story being acted out? (Who wouldn't want this??)

10. How satisfied are you with your ending? Are loose ends more or less tied up. Are you confident that your story will stay with your reader? Could it have ended in any other way?

11. Has your main character been on some kind of journey? A change should have taken place throughout the story for it to carry more impact.

12. Is your work accurate in terms of spelling and punctuation? Have you used adjectives and adverbs *sparingly*?

13. Is your vocabulary strong? (Use a thesaurus or the synonyms function.)

14. Have you done the necessary research?

Well done! You have now written stories in over half the genres outlined in this book! You may already have a favourite, however, there are still four genres to go!

# Young Adult 1

**How writing for young adults is different** You may want to start off by rooting your story in one of the genres we have looked at so far, (supernatural, romance, science fiction or crime,) but try not to make this decision at the outset, rather allow your story to fall into one of them.

There are several ways in which writing for young adults differs from writing from older adults. One of these is the length of the story would be shorter. The others are summarised below:

### Six Golden Rules when Writing for Young Adults

**Age** The age of the protagonist should be similar to that of the intended reader. Teenagers will usually be interested in a book about a character a few years older than them, but generally not the other way around.

**Language** If you have struck a realistic teenage voice, authentic language will follow. Young adults will use words, phrases and slang that adults wouldn't, so, it can often be helpful to listen to this age group in conversation.

**Sensitive Subjects** Many issues are acceptable in terms of what is appropriate for young-adult fiction. However, 13-16 fiction will not actively involve sex or drugs. For 16-20 fiction, there are less bounds in terms of topic; even subjects such as sexuality, abuse, crime and drugs can be written about.

**Preachiness** Nobody wants to be preached at when they are reading fiction. Never is this truer than in writing for young adults. Writers should *raise* questions, rather than answer them. Writer views and opinions may peek through the narrative, but the character voice will feel inauthentic if the narrative becomes patronising.

**Voice** When writing young adult fiction, the voice needs to be immediate, rather than as an adult looking back. A teenage character can recollect their younger years, but is unable to have an adult's wisdom, which can only be gained with hindsight. The writer should be positioned in the teenage mind with no inkling of grown up perspective.

**Hopeful Endings** Readers should be left with hope, if only a glimmer, despite whatever grim action has gone before. Adult stories, whilst dealing with difficult issues, can leave a reader bereft. But in writing for young adults there is a sense of responsibility—not to give warnings, but to allow for what is possible. Readers can be given power and the knowledge that any choices are theirs.

To summarise, when writing young adult fiction, as with all fiction, characters should learn, grow and change during the duration of the story. This should be solely from the events being experienced through their teenage perspective, rather than any adult interjections or hindsight.

This section is going to concentrate on the age group 13-20, and you will probably narrow your age group down further, once you get started on your own story.

[cwb 15.1] **Think about the following and make notes:**

- What can you recall reading when you were in the age group you are about to write for?
- How has the world changed for young people since then?
- What things might we have to consider when writing for this age group?
- What issues do young people of today have in their lives? *Circle the item(s) that you feel most drawn towards to potentially tackle in your story.*

[cwb 15.2] **Decide on the gender, name and age of your protagonist.** Without too much forward planning, free write, detailing the day he or she has had *today.* Allow your character to come to you. The definition of free writing is to allow your pen free rein and to write without consideration. Just see what emerges – the results can be surprising.

*You could address the following as you write:*

- What have you been doing today?
- What other people have featured?
- How have you been feeling?

- What are your plans?
- How has your day been?

This process may allow a potential story to materialise - hopefully the entry you have written may also warrant inclusion or adaptation so it fits into your story.

## Diarising Narrative

Stories do not have to be told in a linear or narrative way. Within this genre, we are going to look at telling story through the writing of diary entries. This practice is known as *epistolary writing.* (This also includes the moving on of narrative through the writing of letters, emails and text messages.)

Diarising a narrative allows the focus to be on specific and meaningful episodes, where a reader can fill in the gaps in between the entries themselves. It enables the reader to really connect with the narrative voice and form an emotional attachment.

Anyone who has ever kept a diary knows that it permits the unleashing of all our thoughts and secrets, even more so because the expectation is that no one else will ever read what we have written.

This process does not have to be day after day. Weeks, months or even years can elapse between diary entries. There can also be a variation in length, tone and content of each entry as there would be in an *actual* diary.

Entries can be given even more depth by being broken down into times.

*5.36 There is no point in just laying here. I might as well get up. Feeling terrified about what is ahead today.*

*6.04 No point trying to eat anything. Can't.*

*8.30 Hairdresser has arrived. Starting to look more presentable.* Etc.

An entire story can be told in this way, or just a section of it, to offer extra depth and a unique dimension.

[cwb 15.3] **Write the first diary entry of your story.**

# Young Adult 2

Read back through your story so far. *(Your first diary entry.)*

[cwb 16.1] **If you haven't already, now is a good time to make some decisions in relation to the following:**

- The overview of your story.
- The structure of the diary entries, (weekly, daily, hourly, sporadic.)
- How you will create tension. (More on this in a moment!)
- The duration your story will span.
- How and where it will end.

[cwb 16.2] **You have already written your opening diary entry. Now write your second entry.**

As you continue with your short story for young adults, I would like you to pay particular attention to another tool we have in our writer's toolbox – tension. This is essential to every story you write and is one of the main reasons your reader will continue reading to the end. Here are some tips to create and sustain tension throughout your story:

**Set up the tension.** Keep saying *no* to your characters, especially your protagonist. Whatever it is they want or need, hold it back.

The best conflict is one that appears insurmountable, so pile difficulties on your characters. Never make their situations easier - always harder. Look at your character's goals, and ask yourself, *What's the worst thing that could happen?* Then take the worst thing a step further.

**Backstory reduces the tension as it provides answers.** Backstory in a tense scene slows the pace but reduces tension, as it allows the reader a breather.

If you must reveal information, you can do it through a quick flash of internal thought or a secondary character's dialogue. Hint at certain details to make the reader want to know more.

Leaving details about a character until later in the story is an effective way to keep your readers intrigued. Don't give them all the answers, just give readers enough so they won't be frustrated.

**Enable the reader to feel emotions along with your characters.** Use your character's internal conflict to its best advantage: abandonment, mistrust, emotional deprivation, dependence, social exclusion, or whatever vulnerability you create.

It does not matter what kind of story you are writing or who your characters are—*a story is feelings.* The more there is at stake for your character, the more emotions he or she will feel about events and situations.

The more challenged or tragic a character appears, the more tension a reader feels on their behalf, and the more a reader cares for them.

*Change* is what increases tension as it keeps the reader reading.

New challenges, new information, new twists, and added complications—all assure extra potential for tension.

[cwb 16.3] **Where is the tension going to be in *your* story?**

How could you increase it? What further obstacles could you put in your character's way?

[cwb 16.4-8] **Continue with your story, diary entry by diary entry.**

Remember that you can bullet point each entry before writing so you know it's content. This is particularly useful when you wish to plan out your next stage before leaving it for the day. Your diary entries do not have to be uniform; they can vary in length and tone and be sporadic in terms of when they are written.

Keep writing until you are approaching your ending, but stopping short of the final diary entry for your story.

This way of epistolic writing will give your story a unique edge. As always, I recommend reading something that uses this approach and aimed at a young adult audience. Two longer texts that spring to mind are *The Secret Diary of Adrian Mole,* and *The Diary of Anne Frank.*

# Young Adult 3

I hope you are finding the writing of narrative using the structure of diary entries interesting and innovative. By its nature, it allows for a close connection between writer, character and reader, with lots of emotional depth.

However, there are limitations on the narrative devices that can be utilised using this method, and the diary structure curtails these devices still further when utilising the teenage perspective.

I have identified these challenges below, along with ways to overcome them.

**Challenges with using a 'Diary' Method of Writing**

**Setting** It is difficult to bring setting to life in the same way we would when writing in the traditional 'narrative' way, where we can engage our reader's senses.

This also applies to the wider sense of setting - describing the weather, for example. We can overcome this by offering 'extremes' to our readers in just one line.

E.g. *It was pitch black in there, I wasn't going in* (extreme sensory,) or *it has chucked it down all day* (extreme weather,) *I wasn't able to go out*, or *I got yelled at today for my room being a tip.* (extreme emotion.)

Teenagers often swing to 'extremes' anyway - falling in love is often all-encompassing, setbacks of any kind are the end of the world and anyone in authority is often seen as *the enemy*!

**Character Viewpoint** The act of diarising means you are automatically in first person narrative, and because of the outpouring associated with keeping a diary, this method of writing brings the viewpoint even closer.

Whilst great for increasing emotional connection, there are limitations on showing what is going on for the other characters. We can deal with this by allowing the diary entries to reflect on character interactions.

E.g. *Dad drove me nuts today. One minute he's never at home and always out with his stupid new girlfriend, and the next, he's constantly here, on my case and hammering on my door.*

*Today he was saying that he's worried about me. He reckons I'm spending too much time on my own and I should invite friends around more. Chance would be a fine thing.*

Even though we are not in the character's father's viewpoint, we get a sense of his character, as well as his life and concerns through the main character's viewpoint.

**Dialogue** There is also less scope for the inclusion of dialogue using the diary method. It can still be done, but in an imagined or recounted way.

For example:

*I couldn't believe how awful he was to me today. This is what he said:*

*Him: Are you a stalker or something?*

*Me: No, why do you say that?*

*Him: You always seem to be around.*

*Me: I'm not, honest.*

*Him: Go away. You creep me out.*

*One of his awful friends: It's probably her who took your iPad. Then they all laughed.*

*Me: No, it wasn't. Then I walked off. I was sure I was blushing or something. Really, I think he was only being rotten to me because all his creepy friends were around.*

## Challenges with Writing for a YA Audience

**Character Perspective** When writing as adults, but seeing the world through the eyes of a young person, it's difficult to prevent adult hindsight from creeping in.

'Warm-up' exercises prior to sitting down at our stories can enable us to capture something of our younger selves through free-writing – really concentrating on the era we were in as teenagers and the mindset we had prior to gaining adult wisdom.

**Language** Young people seem to have a language of their own. Words are invented and unique to their generation. If possible, try to listen to how teens relate in as authentic a setting as possible, even if it is just watching TV shows or reading magazines which are aimed at this age group. An example would be:

*I'm feeling a bit meh today. Dad tried to have bants with me earlier but I looked at him as if to say, yeah whatever. Life used to be sik – obvs if Ollie noticed me, everything would be awesome.*

Or in textspeak: *gonna b l8* or *where ru?*

However, when using any of this type of language in our writing, we should remember that many 'adopted' words change and become outdated rapidly.

**Issues, Events and Experiences** Many teen issues are universal over time, such as affairs of the heart, spots, exam pressures and being at that 'in-between' age.

We should do research into issues that have changed, nowadays teens are entrenched in social media, also young people today face issues older generations didn't, such as cyber-bullying, on-line gambling addiction, e-cigarettes and on-line dating.

E.g. He *said he'd add me on Snapchat, I keep opening the app and he hasn't. Lizzie has though, she's posted nasty things on all the photos I've uploaded and there's laughing emojis from all her friends. I've googled how to block them – I can't take it anymore.*

If I had written a passage like the above twenty years ago, much of the terminology would have been nonsensical!

## Ending your Story

Look back over the notes you made on your thoughts as you started your story, about where it might end.

Perhaps you have stayed true to this ending, or maybe your character has deviated along an alternative course which often happens during the writing process.

[cwb 17.1] **Jot some bullet points of what your ending will contain, before writing your final diary entry(ies) to bring the story to its conclusion**.

Keep the following points in mind as you plan and draft your ending:

- We have a responsibility to ensure justice/comeuppance.
- When writing for this age group, we should aim for uplift and hope.
- We must try not to be preachy and allow our adult wisdom to creep in.

## Finally ...

At the editing stage of your young adult's story, <u>read through your story six times</u>. At each of the six read-throughs, focus on each of these challenges in turn:

1. **Setting** Use some 'extreme' sentences to describe setting.
2. **Character Viewpoint** Use reflection to portray alternative viewpoint.
3. **Dialogue** Use recollections or imagined conversations.
4. **Character Perspective** Can you say that you haven't allowed adult hindsight to creep in?
5. **Language** Have you checked that the language you are using is authentic?
6. **Issues, events and experiences**. Have you done enough research to make the experiences *real?*

Consider on each read through whether you have found each aspect a challenge, and look at the advice offered on how to overcome each challenge.

It might also be advantageous at this editing stage to get a younger reader to look over the near-completed story, whilst asking them, *is this how a younger person would speak, think and feel?*

Have you got a variety of **tone, emotion and entry length** to reflect the mind of an adolescent?

The usual editing process should also be applied.

# Fantasy 1

Below, I have collated the questions I hear most often in relation to the reading and writing of fantasy fiction.

**What is fantasy?** Fantasy is, (according to the Oxford Dictionary,) *A genre of imaginative fiction involving magic and adventure, especially in a setting other than the real world.*

**How does it differ from science fiction?** It differs from science fiction in that it is totally imaginative; beyond nature and the laws of science, though in bookshops and libraries, science fiction and fantasy are often shelved together.

**What is its history?** It is often thought JR Tolkien was a founder author is this genre with *The Hobbit* and *Lord of the Rings,* but in reality, the genre has its roots as early as texts such as *Beowulf* and *Sir Gawain and the Green Knight.*

**What is its appeal to readers and writers?** It can offer a high level of escapism from real life with the immersion of our reader in an imaginative world. At a deeper level, it can appeal to our 'inner child' and allows for the unpacking of human thoughts and feelings.

It can help us make sense of our secret worlds with all the conflicts that may exist within us. (e.g. the desire to control, be rich, acquire something or someone we want, or be powerful in some way.)

**What does it deal with?** At its core, fantasy is nearly always a story about humanity, even when its characters are mythical. It deals with the innate 'stuff' of humans such as challenges, relationships, emotions, flaws, courage, victories and defeats.

**What elements should it contain to be classified as fantasy?** To be classed as fantasy, a story needs to be make-believe and beyond the realms of possibility. It may not be of this space and time, and contain a magic and power outside ourselves. Ultimately, it will be an adventure.

**What are the tropes of fantasy fiction?** First, I shall define the term, 'trope.' It is a commonly used element contained within a genre.

So, in romantic fiction, a trope might be a love triangle or a forced separation. In children's fiction, a trope might be good outcomes or a happily ever after. In fantasy fiction, here are some tropes:

Humans who can fly, casting of spells, potions, elves/goblins/d warves, a chosen one, a portal, a quest for an artefact, villains seeking world power, unicorns, dragons, mythical beasts, etc.

If you decide to use one or more of these tropes in your story, find a fresh and innovative way of doing it.

You may already have an idea for a fantasy story, but if not, here are some initial story ideas you could use or adapt:

- The process of visualisation makes things happen.
- Each person's spirit is connected to a particular animal. Meeting them evokes a power.
- An underwater world comes to the surface.
- She thought she was human.
- He is so powerful, he can inhabit someone else.
- A flock of birds spells out a secret.
- She can make a potion that can make anyone do anything.

**Five key elements your story must have**

[cwb 18.1] **Make notes under the headings below.**

You can do them in any order. Your story may emerge from any of them as a starting point. Try not to overthink, but allow your imagination free rein.

**A World** A key element of fantasy is 'other worldliness' – perhaps a portal will exist to reach it?

- How does your world look, smell, feel and sound? (Landscape, buildings, climate.)
- What is the history of your world?
- How does society operate? (Class, hierarchy, democracy.)

**Characters** Perhaps human, but if not, should embody human characteristics and emotions.

- Who is your central character?
- Who will be their allies/enemies?
- At the outset of the story, what are the goals and objectives of each character?

**Magic** A magic system should exist that cannot be in force in the real world.

- What is your magic and where does it come from?
- What is its cost or sacrifice?
- What is its danger?

**Adventure** Fantasy fiction should take a reader on a journey remote from everyday life.

- What dangers will your character face?
- What joys and rewards might be possible?
- What changes will take place?

**Conflict** Conflicts can be over arching, and external or internal.

- How does character action result in conflict?
- What power struggle will be evident in your story?
- What is at stake?

[cwb 18.1] **You may wish to use the prompts below for character creation, and you may wish to look for a fantastical picture online, or describe a world borne out of your imagination.**

- Name/Age
- Appearance
- Home/Family
- Background
- Special Talent
- Prized Possession
- Happiest Memory
- What makes them angry?
- Biggest Dream
- Internal Monologue

[cwb 18.2] **Decide on what your main 'other-worldly' aspect is going to be: character, setting, super-powerful attribute, key object and put the emphasis on that as you write your story opening.**

[cwb 18.3] **Plot out the order of the rest of your story using a story arc.**

# Fantasy 2

I am now going to introduce another approach to planning and writing – interweaving text. This involves the seamless building of narrative

Narrative comprises setting, back story, character action, interiority, dialogue and emotion, then blending them together so there is a balance between them.

To pick these elements apart, I would advise photocopying a page or two from a story, preferably a fantasy story, and using different colour pens to pick out instances of the aforementioned narrative elements and study how they have been interwoven amongst one another. For example, how does dialogue, interiority and character action fit together?

An example of a short story in the fantasy genre, freely available online is *One True Love* by Malinda Lo.

Too much emphasis on one, (for instance, a full page of setting or back story,) can interrupt the reading experience, but the *interweaving* of them is more likely to enable reader immersion in the story.

Read back what you have written so far – your planning and your story opening. You may have used the character prompts to get to know your key characters and hear their voices. You may have also plotted your entire short story out on the story arc and be raring to get onto the next scene!

[cwb 19.1] **Use the 'interweaving text' sub-headings below to plan the narrative aspects of setting for <u>your second scene</u>.**

You will be focussing on setting, back story, character action, interiority, dialogue and emotion.

**Setting** As much sensory detail as possible.

**Back Story** What has led the character to the point they are currently at? This might be prior to where your story has started.

**Character Action** What will your character be *doing* as your scene progresses?

**Interiority** What will be going through your character's mind? Remember, you can only ever know the thoughts of your viewpoint character.

**Dialogue** Give an overview of what your characters will say to each other.

**Emotion** How are your characters feeling? This is what helps to create reader/character connection.

[cwb 19.2] **Once you have written this plan, draft your second scene** with a beginning, middle and end, interweaving the narrative elements you have decided on.

[cwb 19.3-19.10] **Continue with this process**, scene after scene – stopping short of your end scene.

Enjoy really letting your imagination run free!

# Fantasy 3

Read back through your story so far. You should have now reached the point where you will write your ending.

Make a list of four different ways it could end. Even if you have a very good idea already – it is a great exercise to think outside the box and consider other possibilities – no matter how far-fetched. In fact, in the realms of fantasy, perhaps the more far-fetched, the better!

[cwb 20.1] **Choose one of your endings and make notes under the headings below:**

- What challenges have your characters faced – how has this changed them?
- How have relationships altered over the course of the story?
- What is the range of emotion portrayed throughout the story?
- What fundamental flaws have your characters displayed?
- Has courage been shown? How?
- What victories have been won?
- What defeats have been suffered?
- Has morality been addressed in any way?

- What has been learned by your characters?
- How do you want your reader to be left feeling at the end of your story?

[cwb 20.2] **Use the same planning approach you have used throughout the story so far to plan your ending and then write the first draft of it.** [cwb 20.3]

Once you have done that, it's time for the edit. Below, I have outlined the process I use for my own writing. Follow this process yourself.

## Draft One

- At this stage, you are *telling the story to yourself.*
- Get the story out of your head and onto the page. You can worry about spelling, layout and punctuation later.
- The level of planning you achieved prior to starting your story will make this stage easier.
- Don't edit anything at this stage. Editing cancels out creativity.
- Keep going forward, one scene at a time, until you have finished.

## Draft Two

- Has your story started in the right place? Writers often launch in too early, giving too much explanation or back-story rather than beginning at a point of action.
- Omit episodes or characters that are not adding anything to your story, nor moving it forwards.

- Wherever possible, ensure that you are 'showing' rather than 'telling.'

## Draft Three

- Go through your story from the beginning through to the end, (on screen.) Do this in one sitting if you can.
- Check every word is the best it can be, using the 'synonyms' function on your computer or a thesaurus. Every word counts.
- Reading should be an active process – have you enabled the reader to 'fill in gaps' themselves sometimes?
- Check all your scenes have a beginning, middle and end.

## Draft Four

- Now print out your entire story and annotate with a pen. You will notice things on the page, you didn't on the screen.
- Ensure consistency in terms of tense – it is so easy to slip in and out of past and present tense.
- Ensure consistency of viewpoint and character details.
- Beware of overwriting. Of being too wordy.
- Check spelling, grammar and punctuation.
- Are there any incidences in your story that you need to improve – where perhaps it is important to check your facts through further research.
- Can any scenes be improved with more sensory detail? Go beyond the visual.
- Return to the screen version of your story and make all the necessary corrections.

**Draft Five**

- Read the story aloud, keeping all the aforementioned points in mind and editing as necessary.
- Pay particular attention to the dialogue. Is it authentic?
- This out loud reading will highlight any general clumsiness and interruption in the flow.

**Then ...**

- If possible, get someone else to read it. A fresh pair of eyes will always notice things which you have missed.

**Congratulations! Your story should now be the best it can be!**

I suggest you now revisit your earlier stories. They will have gone 'cold,' in terms of your memory of creating them, and apply the same editing process.

# Historical 1

For the historical fiction genre, you will tell your story in an epistolic way, as in the young adult genre, however, you will use letter writing as your device for moving the story forwards. This method of communicating would have been largely used in the era in which you will set your story.

[cwb 21.1] **Consider the following:**

- What historical fiction have you enjoyed reading?
- What historical events interest and intrigue you?
- What does the term historical fiction mean to you?
- How much time needs to elapse for something to be classed as history?

**Now, let's take a closer look.**

Historical fiction is a genre which exists in an already-lived-t hrough era. Whilst elements can be imaginatively recreated, like situations and characters, this is a genre that calls for more research, and accuracy of certain elements than other genres, as a proportion of what is told will be rooted in fact.

As a writer, your job is to tell a story, therefore whilst historical facts need to be accurate, readers have picked your story up to be entertained, rather than educated, so consider this balance as you write.

### *How much time should have elapsed for an era or event to be classed as history?*

There is no definitive answer to this. Possibilities include:

- When something has happened and is in the past.
- When no one is still living from the time to present a biased opinion.
- When a significant time has elapsed – e.g. 50 or 100 years.
- An actual famous, interesting and notable event.
- When acceptance or learning, after an incident, has occurred.
- When society has moved on from a time in terms of values, norms and culture.

Your job as the author of a historical story is to ensure all elements that should be contained within a short story, such as character, tension, etc, as previously discussed, whilst authentically bringing the past to life, are included.

### [cwb 21.2] Decide on a premise for your short story. I have made some suggestions below to help you.

- Letters between a serving WW1 soldier and his sweetheart.
- Letters between an evacuated WW2 child and his mother.
- Letters between an unmarried expectant mother in the 50s

and her parents.
- Letters between two pen friends in the 60s.
- Letters between two estranged family members in a bygone era.

Make notes in response to the emboldened headings below to help plan your story. At this point, some research may be necessary.

[cwb 21.3] **A compelling plot** The sequence of events that make up your story should tie in with historical events. For example, if your story is set in 1941, you would need the backdrop of WW2.

What events will occur in your story? What will the historical backdrop be?

[cwb 21.4] **Multi-dimensional characters that the reader cares about** Characters should behave in keeping with the historic time you are presenting so it may be necessary to research societal norms, attitudes, and beliefs. As a writer, you must show that they are a character of the past through their dress, language and occupation.

Make notes on your characters. You may find it helpful to use one of the character profiles given earlier in the course? Ensure your characters are in keeping with the historic period.

[cwb 21.5] **A sense of place and atmosphere** Bringing time and place to life, using the senses. E.g. the pounding of hooves, the glow of candlelight, food kept in the pantry.

*Sight:*
*Sound:*
*Smell:*
*Taste:*
*Feel:*

[cwb 21.6] **Conflict** The conflict, and reasons behind it, should be realistic for the time and place you are writing about.

Internal and external conflicts that will be faced by your characters:

[cwb 21.7] **A journey or change** As with all stories, the characters must have evolved.

How will your characters have changed at the end of the story, compared to the beginning?

[cwb 21.8] **A sense of resolution** When ending your story, it will be necessary to consider aspects such as societal expectation, family, religion, law and politics.

How might your conflict be resolved?

[cwb 21.9] **As well as the seamless interweaving of narrative elements, you need to bear in mind the everyday life faced by your characters:**
Travel:
Food:
News:
Communities:

Costs of Living:
Landscape:
Class Arrangements:
Buildings:
Weather:
Military Organisation:
Availability of Commodities:
Disease:

[cwb 21.10] **A strong opening** Write your story opening – the first letter in the sequence. This should take readers straight into the time you are writing about. Here is an example of an opening letter to offer a flavour of the tone you could aim for:

Dear Arthur,

When you read this, you will be thousands of miles away. I hope you are safe. I keep trying to talk to you inside my head and wish you could somehow hear me.

I am looking at the beautiful bunch of roses you gave to me to say goodbye. They are still as alive and beautiful as our love. I smell them everywhere and they remind me of you, not that you are ever far from my thoughts.

Life has come between us; the war, my parents and the fact that we met each other too late. I cannot marry Francis. You are the only man I want to marry. Please come home soon.

With all my love, Sarah

Dating each letter is a good device to show passage of time and allow readers to infer what is happening and fill in the gaps between each letter, in a similar way to the diary entries you wrote.

An online example of something you could read in keeping with this genre is *Birdcage Walk* by Helen Dumnore.

# Historical 2

Read back over your notes and planning so far. You should have written the first letter from your series of letters. Read this aloud in order to *hear* your character's voice.

You may wish to plan your entire story before writing. You can plot out your entire series of letters at once, or you may want to plan them prior to writing them.

By now, you will probably have established whether you are a plotter or a discovery writer – a writer that writes with little or no prior preparation, often referred to as a 'pantser.'

[cwb 22.1] **Write the reply to your first letter.** After writing the first draft, again, read it aloud.

Telling your story in an epistolic way allows for more freedom as you can equally get into the viewpoint of your second character. You can choose what to add in and leave out, selecting the most interesting elements, whilst allowing for lapses of time in between, similar to when you were diarising your story.

Within the size constraints of the short story, you are probably best keeping your letter exchange between just two characters, unless there is good reason for adding a third.

[cwb 22.2-6] **Keep going with your series of letters,** stopping before you come to the final one.

# Historical 3

By now you will have written a series of letters between your two characters, stopping short of the final letter in your series.

Read through your story so far in order to re-familiarise yourself with it, and to hear your character's voices once more.

One of the exciting things about being a writer, which I hope you are finding as well, is how the characters begin to live within you as you are creating their stories.

Whilst writing can be an insular occupation, you are never lonely and will always have your characters for company!

[cwb 23.1] **Write the final letter in your story, planning the content and tone beforehand if this is your process**. Ensure this final letter ties up any loose ends and leaves a sense of resolution.

Type your letters, if you haven't already, and then methodically begin to go through the editing checklist below. It deals specifically with the genre of historical fiction.

[cwb 23.2] *Consider the following questions as you edit your short story:*

- Does your story contain a conflict from the outset?
- Have you dated each letter, showing the passage of time between each one?
- In your letters, have you given historical context to show what is happening around your character's situations?
- Have you checked any historical facts?
- Have you been able to include some character emotion as you write? Remember this is what ensures your reader will care.
- Have you been able to show how different life was to how it is now, in the time period you have chosen?
- How have things changed at the end of your story to how they were at the beginning?
- Are the language choices you have made authentic with the era in which you have set your story?
- Do each of your characters have their own agendas and sub plots which they are pursuing?
- Are your character's voices distinct from one another?
- Have you checked your work for factors such as spelling, grammar, repetition, consistency, overuse of adjectives and adverbs?
- Have you read it aloud?
- How are you wanting your reader to feel when they have read your story? Have you achieved this?

# Comedy 1

Comedy is the final genre to be explored in the course; a word of warning though – writing comedy is not as easy as it first appears, although perhaps I am merely speaking as a crime thriller writer!

Perhaps the main difficulty is that there are many factors that can affect what a reader might find amusing such as age, background, status, life experience, culture and gender.

Let's begin with a definition of comedy and its effect...

Comedy is designed to be entertaining and escapist. It can alter a person's mood in a positive way by making them laugh at something outside themselves.

[cwb 24.1] **The best way into this is to consider, personally, what do *you* find funny?**

You might like to think of the *type* of humour you think you have. It may also be useful to reflect on incidents and experiences which have left a humorous mark, and books and films which have made you laugh.

Of course, what individuals find funny varies from person to person, but if you stay close to something you as the writer would be amused by in your writing, you won't go far wrong.

As comedy writers, our best tools are dysfunctional character traits, (aka flaws,) and then we can use situations to best present a conflict. An example here could be that of Basil Fawlty, whose overriding negative character trait is rudeness. The humour is brought about as his flaws are at odds with how a hotel proprietor is supposed to act.

Being a flawed person is usually at the heart of comedy. All characters have flaws, it's what makes them multi-dimensional. We can invent original characters by drawing on our own shortcomings, (habits, failings and weaknesses) and those of our family and friends. (Mine would be my terrible sense of geographical direction!)

[cwb 24.2] **Use the prompts below to develop your central character.**

You will start with a central flaw, then working outwards.

1. Decide firstly on the character defect(s) you will use. (Cowardice, pomposity, lateness, unreliability, infidelity.)
2. Next, invent your main character basics: name, age, occupation, background/family, appearance.
3. Their most annoying habit.
4. What has happened in their life to exacerbate the flaw you have chosen – why are they the way they are?
5. Something they have done that they cringe to recall.

6. Any plans they have which could be scuppered?
7. What is the funniest thing that could happen to this character to cause as much mayhem as possible?

Next you will invent a second character that is somehow at odds with the one you have just created.

To use Bridget Jones as an example, her character flaws are that she is insecure, chaotic and ditzy. Mark Darcy is one of the main secondary characters whose main personality traits are confident successful and knowledgeable. The contrast between them, in part, generates the humour.

[cwb 24.3] **Use the prompts below to create a second character in your story.**

Should you need further characters in your story, use the prompts as many times as you need to. What character traits will this character possess which are at odds with your main character?

1. Invent your secondary character basics: name, age, occupation, relationship to main character, background/family, appearance.
2. Their most annoying habit.
3. What do they secretly think about the main character?
4. Something they would like to change.
5. What plans does s/he have that may or may not contrast with the main characters?
6. What is the funniest thing that could happen to this character to cause as much mayhem as possible?

Now that you have at least two of your characters and a setting, jot down some story premises where you can create a comedy scenario.

## [cwb 24.4] Your Opening Setting

You will now decide on the opening setting for your characters. In comedy, *place* is another aid for humour, again using a setting that is at odds with the character.

For example, Basil Fawlty owns a hotel where manners and a warm welcome would be the norm. The comedy is created by his rudeness to guests.

- Where will your story start?
- How can you ensure that your setting is 'at odds' with your character?
- Make some notes that also offer some sensory information you can include when you draft your story.

## [cwb 24.5] Your Opening Scene.

- Make sure you introduce your main character and the setting.
- Give your reader a clue that they can expect something funny – set up the conflict you have created between your character in their relationships, setting and circumstances.
- Use the elements of 'a good story opening' that we have explored earlier in the course.

As with all the other genres, reading or even watching comedy whilst you are working within the genre will be really helpful and will also put you in the right mindset to be funny!

It is difficult to recommend a story for you as we all differ in our humour but the aforementioned Bridget Jones books are certainly among my favourites!

# Comedy 2

As you approach the end of the final genre, you will write during this course, I would now like to deal with the concept of 'show, don't tell.'

This is another tool you have available within your writers toolbox – one that should be kept in mind at all stages of writing, and particularly effective when reflected on at the editing stage.

Although you have carried out some editing on each of your stories already, I would suggest that now some time has elapsed for them to 'go cold,' you will have very fresh eyes to revisit them all, and therefore in a good place to consider whether you have 'shown,' rather than 'told.'

*Show, don't tell* is a technique used in all types of writing, enabling readers to experience a narrative through character action, sensory language, dialogue, description and thoughts. The reader has the opportunity to interpret details in the text, making reading a more active process.

For example, instead of describing a character as short, we can show them being on tiptoe to reach for something from a low shelf. Another example might be that instead of stating that a character is upset, we can have another character passing them a tissue.

Where a writer does this well, the reader can be in the moment, feeling and experiencing events alongside characters. Below are some examples.

**Using Character Action** *Continuing along the lane, her pace quickened with each step. She kept looking behind, hearing her heartbeat thudding in her ears.*

Here, the emotion of fear is conveyed through the character's walk. It is not necessary to say, 'she was scared.'

**Using Sensory Language** *The smell took her right back. It was the aftershave he'd worn when they'd been dating.*

In this instance, smell conveys nostalgia. 'She missed him' is not needed.

**Using Dialogue** *"Thomas Clifford," Mum stood at the door with her hands on her hips. "Get in here this instant!"*

The reader can infer that Mum is angry.

**Using Description** *He cradled the guitar in his arms like a lover. Together, they had created history.*

That the character loves his guitar and is proud of something, is obvious.

**Using Internal Thought** "It's fine, honestly." Dan folded his arms. *You'll get what's coming to you ...*

Dan is planning something, and things are *not* fine. We are *shown* this, rather than *told.*

Continue from the opening which you wrote in the last session.

[cwb 25.1-5] **Plan each of your scenes,** using a bullet pointing approach first. Remember to keep the humour alive – we can increase this further at editing stage.

Stay focused on the elements that will ensure this: character flaws, characters being at odds with one another, their settings or their circumstances.

[cwb 25.6-10] **Write each of your scenes out as your first draft.** Give each scene within your story its *own* beginning, middle and end. Also aim for 'show, don't tell.' Perhaps you could use one or more of the following in each of your scenes.

**Character Action:** Have your main character taking a walk and showing through how s/he is walking, how they are feeling.

**Sensory Language:** Have your main character hearing, seeing, smelling, tasting or touching something which makes them recall something from the past. What effect does it have on them?

**Dialogue:** Engage one character in a conversation with another character. Show their mood through what is being said.

**Description:** Use a possession belonging to one of your characters to portray something of your character's personality – show how he feels about it.

**Internal Thought:** Through your character's thinking, give detail of something they are planning and their emotion about it.

Remember to imagine that your story could be acted out. After all, why wouldn't you want to be the author behind the next big comedy series or romcom!

# Comedy 3

It is now time to complete your final story of the course, before taking the next steps with the work you have produced .

Read through your story so far - you should be at the point of writing your comedy story's ending.

Before you start, let's consider how a reader should feel when they reach the end of a funny story. Ideally they will reach the end and feel entertained, amused, uplifted, satisfied, wanting more of the same and eager to recommend your story to others. Decide how you will end your story to achieve this.

Bearing in mind what makes a 'good' story ending, as considered earlier in the course, keep the comedy aspect at the forefront of your writing.

[cwb 26.1] **Write to the end of your story.**

Let it 'go cold' for a few days - time away from your story is essential to achieve detachment. When you read it over, try to see it through a reader's eyes. Imagine the parts where they would be amused. At these points, make it even funnier.

[cwb 26.2] **Below are some prompts to help you reflect on the comedy you have written.**

- Intensify the conflict between the characters and the main character with their setting.
- If anything more can go wrong, allow this to happen!
- Ask yourself what the funniest thing is that could happen at this given moment.
- If possible, read your story aloud to a trusted listener or get a trusted reader to read it – do they find the intended parts amusing?

# Getting your Work into Print

Here's the most exciting chapter of them all, and no doubt the one you have been waiting for! As writers, we all have our own definition of success. For some, it might be that family and friends enjoy our stories. For others, it might be having our stories published in a magazine, whilst some writers may aspire to production of a full-length short story collection with mass-market appeal.

Short stories are great for building up a 'CV' of writing successes, which will do wonders for your confidence as a writer and make you an attractive proposition for publishers.

Once you have edited and re-edited your stories until they are at the best possible standard you can get them, you next need to get the presentation right.

**Font** Make sure the font is legible, (12 point is usual,) and consistent throughout your novel, use Aerial or Times New Roman. Text is double spaced throughout and left aligned, (not fully justified.)

**Margins** Standard margin size on A4 is 2.54cm on all sides.

**Pages** All pages should be numbered, with a header set, (in a smaller font size than the main text,) with your name and the story title in italics. This would not be the case if you are entering your story into a short story competition as the entries are usually anonymous.

**Layout** Paragraphs do not need a gap between them. Only leave a space if there is a change of section. There is no need to use * to indicate a section break unless it occurs at the top or bottom of a page. Never indent the first line after a section break. The beginning of all other paragraphs are indented. This includes paragraphs that consist of dialogue.

Now that you have got your presentation nailed, it is time to consider who might like to see it and enjoy the wonderful stories you have written. There is no feeling like seeing your work in print. Here are some ideas to make this a reality:

### Subscribe to a regular writing publication

I always recommend subscribing to Writing Magazine because of the amount of short story competitions they run. They also offer information about other national and international magazine submission opportunities, and details of anthologies that are inviting inclusion.

### Competitions

As already mentioned, creative writing competitions are a wonderful way of learning to work to deadlines and word count constraints. They will not only build your confidence as a writer but also your writing 'CV'. A quick internet search will give you comprehensive details of all that is available, locally, nationally and internationally.

**Literary Agents**

There are few literary agents that would consider taking on a debut short story collection writer, so if you are ultimately wanting to find one to represent you and negotiate with publishers on your behalf, you are best building up your CV of short story successes first, before approaching them with a full short story collection.

It is worth mentioning that it is as difficult to get a literary agent as it is a publisher. But once you have one, it is much easier to secure a publishing contract.

**Publishers**

The publication of short stories is more niche than that of full length novels. Therefore you will need to identify publishers who accept short stories and the Writers and Artist's Yearbook, updated annually, is a good place to start. I would advise that you trawl through the listings to check if they are willing to accept un-agented submissions as many will state 'no unsolicited submissions.'

**Magazines and Newspapers**

There are many opportunities to get your short stories into magazines, particularly for women's fiction. In the UK, magazines like Prima, Woman's Weekly, Take a Break and many more pay quite well for short pieces of fiction. Newspapers like the People and the Daily Mail often accept short story submissions. It is another excellent way to build up your list of successes.

## Anthologies of Short Stories

You could join with other writers to create a themed short story collection, which has been contributed too by several authors and split the profits. This idea leads us into…

## Independent Publishing

You could opt to cut out the gatekeepers, (agents, competitions and publishers,) and get your work straight in front of your readers, and also keep hold of more of the profit. For this I recommend Kindle Direct Publishing, (and enrolling into Kindle Unlimited which pays a 70% royalty).

You can produce your collection as a paperback and as an e-book. Here are some things to consider before you make this decision:

- Your writing must be edited and polished. (Preferably professionally.)
- Consider having the book cover professionally designed.
- You will need to research the formatting process.
- You should be prepared to have a budget for Amazon ads and Facebook ads to get your work in front of readers. (A steep learning curve awaits you here but there is lots of

help out there to learn all about it!)
- You can order a box of author copies to give/sell directly to your family and friends and sell at any launch events or promotions you organise.

[cwb 27.1] **Research and make notes around the initial steps you will take towards getting your work into print.**

Good luck! (Keep me posted!)

# Author Platform

As you approach the end of this short story course, you may be thinking about 'living as a writer,' and immersing yourself as much as possible in the world of writing. An author platform has two elements; the *online* element which comprises social media, blogging and having a website.

Then there is the *offline* element which comprises real, physical writing communities you can belong to, such as writing groups and writer's circles or literary events you can attend.

**Social Media**

There are many social media platforms, (e.g. Pinterest, Instagram, LinkedIn,) but I would suggest that the two that are most worthy of being concentrated on for writers are Facebook and Twitter.

Facebook is great for networking and building community. It is the platform where people over forty seem to mostly congregate which may or may not equates with your target readership.

It is great for creating events, advertising books, sharing publishing successes, and posing writing-related questions. If starting out as a writer on Facebook, I would suggest 'friending' as many other writers as you can and joining a couple of Facebook groups which interest you.

Twitter is good for building your 'writing brand' and showcasing your authority in a particular area. You can follow anyone, and anyone can follow you.

The demographic is slightly younger than Facebook, probably age thirty to fifty. If starting out as a writer on Twitter, I would suggest following other writers, publishers, publications, agents, literary festivals and competitions that interest you.

Social media can be extremely time consuming, and I recommend limiting it to no more than twenty minutes of scrolling through your news feeds each day.

It is effective for learning about submission opportunities, competitions and writing events. It's also a way for writers to support and promote one another.

The rule of thumb is 80/20 – that is eighty percent interacting with other posts and sharing general information about writing, and twenty percent self-promotion.

A prospective publisher would expect you to be on at least one social media platform and be able to use it for advertising your work and to promote events.

## Blogging

This is an excellent way to showcase your writing ability and can be used to educate, inform or inspire others, whilst building a following of potential readers.

Personally I blog on the craft of writing and how to live as a writer, and call my blog 'Writerly Witterings.' Other writers might blog on travel, food or perhaps something related to the type of fiction they write. For example, a romance writer might blog about relationships, and a historical writer might blog about life in the era from which they are writing.

Using keywords throughout a blog can be a great way to bring people to your website and gain interest in something else you can offer, (like your short story collection!)

## Having a Website

A website is the shop window for you as a writer. It should offer information about you, your successes, your news, publications, blog and anything else you have to offer – for example, you might want to make yourself available to speak in front of an audience, or to buddy up with another writer to swap extracts to critique.

I recommend WordPress, as the support is good and the basic websites are free. You can also host your blog here. It tends to be straightforward to set up, which is what you need when you are first starting out.

So now that we have looked at the various ways you can build an online presence as a writer, let us now turn our attention to offline activities.

Literature festivals offer amazing opportunities to network with other writers, attend writing workshops and listen to published writers.

But festivals are often infrequent annual events, usually held in March and October, so open mic, (spoken word) events can offer something more regular, and can build your confidence in terms of putting your work and your writing self out there.

**There are several advantages of attending open mic events:**

- Being able to showcase your work and yourself as a writer.
- Becoming part of a community and network.
- Living as a writer and improving confidence.
- Listening and watching the styles of other writers and becoming more familiar with trends.
- Being less isolated as a writer.

**Nerves can be a problem, below are a few tips for how to overcome them:**

- Know your work is the best it can be.
- Become familiar with the use of a microphone.
- Rehearse it at home, possibly in front of a mirror and time yourself. (Usually you will be given three to five minutes – long enough to read a short story of around a thousand

words.) Note any occasions of stumbling over words.

- Going first can make you feel as though you are getting it out of the way, but by listening to several other writers before it is your turn, you give yourself time to focus outside yourself and get a feel for the theme and content.
- This time can also be used for regulating your breath.

**Whilst reading:**

- Ensure your position is comfortable and the right distance in relation to the microphone.
- Remember to breathe!
- Read your work slowly and clearly, pausing where necessary to allow the words to sink in – overcome the temptation to rush.
- Imagine yourself as a 'vehicle' for your work – as though the words are emerging from behind you and are just travelling through you to meet your audience.
- Look up from your page every so often – look out across your audience.
- Hold a book or a folder containing your work – the shakes will be less obvious. I got these dreadfully the first time!
- Ensure you read a piece where the audience will be in no doubt, where it ends.
- Congratulate yourself afterwards and remember it will not always be so nerve-wracking – all writers have to read for the first time somewhere!

[cwb 28.1] **Decide on one area from either the online or offline activities and make some notes on the first steps you will take.**

# Your Next Writing Steps

Now that you've reached the end of your course, it could be helpful to consider where you go from here. Below are a few suggestions, drawn together from the last few sessions of the book.

- Subscription to a writing magazine – remember these will keep you in the know about opportunities and events, whilst being an excellent source for continued learning.
- Open mic and spoken word nights – a chance for you to gain confidence reading your writing to an audience.
- Developing your on-line author platform – essential but give yourself plenty of time to develop at least one social media platform, a basic website and a blog.
- Attend further courses – look out for workshops at literature festivals and writing days.
- This is a great place to mention the year-long writing courses I offer. Visit https://mariafrankland.co.uk/online-creative-writing-courses/ for more information.
- You may want to aim even higher and consider an OU, BA or MA in Creative Writing or other accredited course. I also have lots of free courses on You Tube.
- Attend literature festivals. They are widely held in March

and October. Packed with workshops and inspirational speakers, they also usually hold a competition and offer networking opportunities.

- Keep making submissions – make a promise to yourself to submit some of your writing to a magazine, newspaper, or competition regularly. Perhaps each month. As mentioned before, this will build up your writing CV.

- Manuscript appraisal – if you have not already done so, consider having your stories professionally critiqued, edited and proofread. Make sure you have got it to the best place you can on your own before you submit it. A writing buddy can be brilliant for peer assessment whereby you can improve each other's work.

- Forming or joining a writing group – writing can be a lonely and solitary activity, therefore joining an established writing group can be an excellent way to stay connected to other writers. It also offers the opportunity to help one another and provide feedback to one another. If there isn't one in your area, consider starting one up of your own.

- Finally, I would like you to formulate three **S.M.A.R.T.** writing-related goals. These could be related to your writing craft or to your professional development. Ensure they are **S**pecific, **M**easurable, **A**ttainable, **R**ealistic and **T**imed. I would love you to share them with me at maria@mariafr ankland.co.uk. Just the act of communicating them offers accountability and will make you more inclined to achieve them!

I wish you all the luck in the world as you near completion of your short story collection. Keep on enjoying the journey and keep me posted. I will be first in the queue for a signed copy – glass of bubbly in hand!

## Before you go....

Join my 'keep in touch' list to receive a free book, and to be kept posted of other freebies, special offers and new releases. Being in touch with other writers is one of the best things about being an author and creative writing teacher.

Visit www.mariafrankland.co.uk to join and receive a free copy of The 7 S.E.C.R.E.T.S. to Achieving your Writing Dreams.

I'd love to know what you thought of Write a Collection of Short Stories in a Year, and always welcome feedback, both positive and not-so-positive. The easiest way to do this is by leaving a review, and you can leave one by revisiting the Amazon product page.

It's great to know what you want more of, or not, as the case may be. It only needs to be a line or three, but also helps other writers find the book.

## Thank you!

This book is derived from a year-long online course which includes video, access to an online support group, further writing tasks and examples, links to further reading and the option of one-to-one support. See https://mariafrankland.co.uk/short-story-writing-course/for more information.

# By the Same Author

**How-to Books for Writers**
Write your Life Story in a Year
Write a Novel in a Year
Write a Collection of Poetry in a Year

**Memoir**
Don't Call me Mum

**Psychological Thrillers**
Left Hanging
The Man Behind Closed Doors
The Yorkshire Dipper
The Last Cuckoo
Hit and Run
The Hen Party
Last Christmas

**Poetry**
Poetry for the Newly Married 40 Something

# Acknowledgements

I'd like to say a huge thank you to my husband, Michael, for his support and expertise in the latter stages of this book.

Thanks also to all the writers who have taken this course over the years, either in the classroom or by distance learning. Your feedback has enabled me to tweak and refine the course, and many of you have become friends too!

Thank you to Prince Henry's Grammar School in Otley for the space and platform for me to offer my creative writing courses, and I also want to acknowledge Leeds Trinity University where I completed my teaching and English degree, and then my Masters in Creative Writing.

These degrees took me to a new level as a writer and enabled me to pass on my own learning through the courses I have written and now offer.

And lastly, can I thank you, the 'student' of this book, for choosing to share your writing journey with me, and for allowing me to share what I know to help you write your own short story collection. It is a true honour and I hope you will keep me posted of your success!

# About the Author

Maria Frankland's life began at 40 when she began making a living from her own writing and became a teacher of creative writing. The springboard into making writing her whole career was made possible by the MA in Creative Writing she undertook at Leeds Trinity University.

The rich tapestry of life with all its turbulent times has enabled her to pour experience, angst and lessons learned into the writing of her novels and poetry. She recognises that the darkest places can exist within family relationships and this is reflected in the domestic thrillers she writes. She strongly advocates the wonderful power and therapeutic properties of writing.

She is a 'born 'n' bred' Yorkshirewoman, a mother of two, and has recently found her own 'happy ever after' after marrying again. Still in her forties, she is now going to dedicate the rest of her working life to writing her own books, whilst inspiring and motivating other writers to achieve their own writing dreams.

**You can connect with me on:**

- https://www.mariafrankland.co.uk
- https://twitter.com/writermaria_f
- https://www.facebook.com/writermariafrank
- https://www.autonomypress.co.uk

**Subscribe to my newsletter:**

- https://mailchi.mp/f69ecf568e7b/writersignup

Printed in Great Britain
by Amazon